Hand-Drawn Vintage-Style Art

A Nostalgic Walk Through The

Four Seasons

I0086798

Wendy A. Yessler

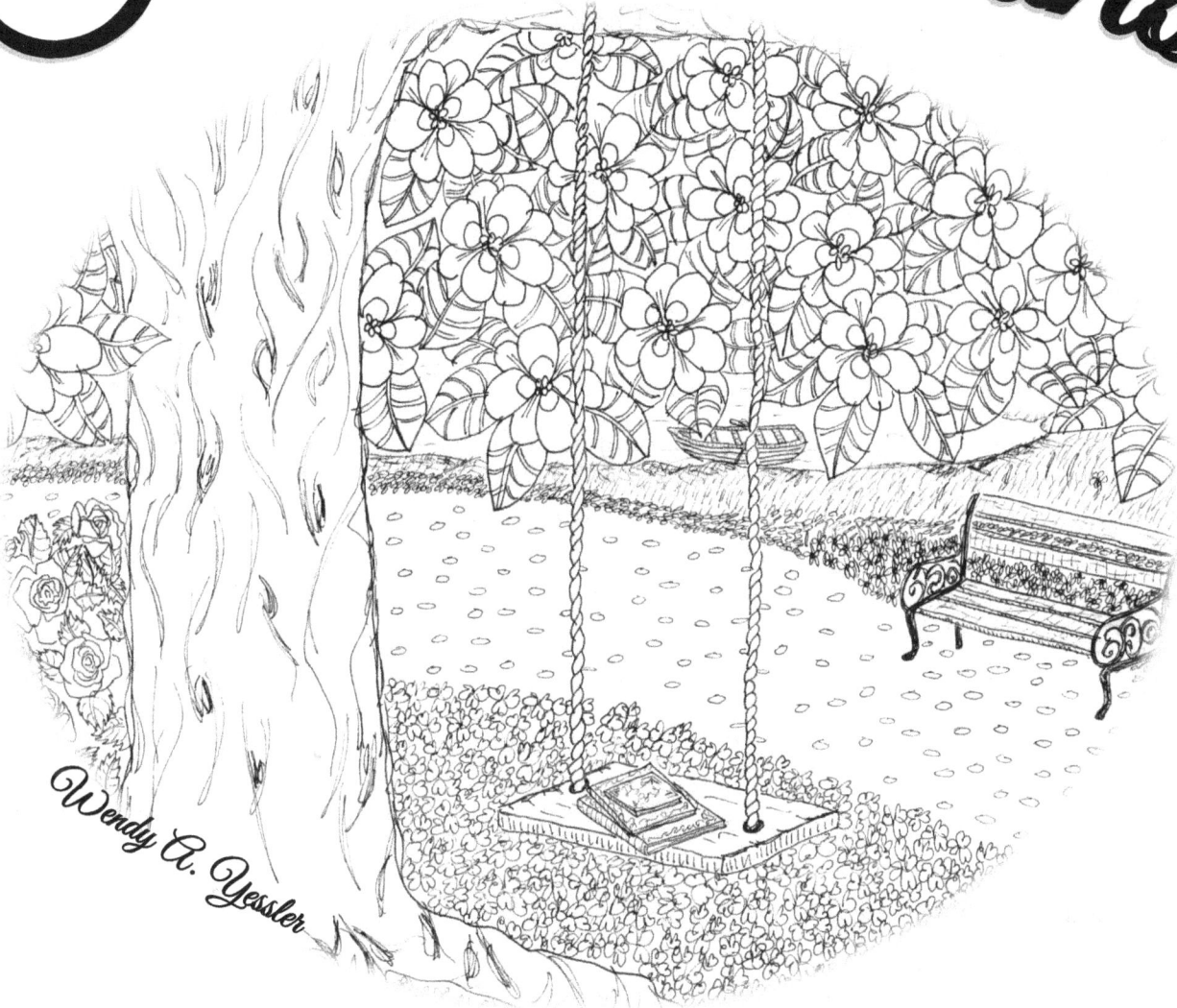

A Coloring Book For Reminiscing

Aliza Batel
Fine Arts Publishing

A Nostalgic Walk Through the *Four Seasons:* A Coloring Book for Reminiscing
Cover design and art By Wendy A. Yessler
Aliza Batel, Fine Arts Publishing

Author can be found on:

Facebook search as Wendy A. Yessler Art & Life Design
                 or https://www.facebook.com/Aliza.Batel/
Instagram @WendyYessler
EyeEm.com: https://www.eyeem.com/u/alizabatel
Society6.com: https://society6.com/alizabatel

The author would like to see your finished pictures. Please post them on the author's Facebook page, along with your comments.

All rights reserved. No part of this book may be reproduced or transmitted by any form or by any means, electronic or mechanical, including photocopy, recording, or any information storage or retrieval system, without prior written consent from the author.

Scripture quotations are from the New King James Version of the Bible. Copyright ©1990, 1985, 1983 by Thomas Nelson, Inc.

NOTE: The pages of this book are suitable for colored pencils, markers and a variety of other media. To help prevent bleed-through, place a loose sheet of paper between the pages when coloring.

Copyright© 2017 by Wendy A. Yessler
All Rights Reserved.
ISBN-13: 978-0692877722
ISBN-10: 069287772X

Contact @ WAY.Art.LifeDesign@gmail.com

ACKNOWLEDGEMENTS

I would like to recognize my grandmother, the late Thelma Stroup Harmon, an accomplished artist who was known for her art in Southern Maryland and the Baltimore-Washington Metropolitan areas. She gave me my first art lessons and inspired me to explore my artistic abilities.

Also deserving of recognition is Judi Eaton Mori, my high school art teacher, friend, and one time neighbor: for always believing in me, as well as her enthusiasm and encouragement to be limitless in advancing my artistic abilities.

I would like to thank my daughter, Nanette, for listening to my ideas, reviewing my work, and giving me input, as well as encouraging me; my son, Nathan, for encouraging me and giving me input; my spiritual son, Manuel, for his encouragement and for his ideas for the toymaker picture and the shepherd; my friend, Julia, for her idea of the apple picker, her enthusiasm and encouragement, as well as her input; my husband, Bobby, for believing I could do this.

Special thanks to Merethe Liljedahl for her generosity and the use of most of the fonts for the pages of reflection.

Finally, I would like to thank all those who have seen this project in process and have encouraged me through their enthusiasm.

To everything *there is* a season,
A time for every purpose under heaven:

A time to be born,
And a time to die;
A time to plant,
And a time to pluck *what is* planted;
A time to kill,
And a time to heal;
A time to break down,
And a time to build up;
A time to weep,
And a time to laugh;
A time to mourn,
And a time to dance;
A time to cast away stones,
And a time to gather stones;
A time to embrace,
And a time to refrain from embracing;
A time to gain,
And a time to lose;
A time to keep,
And a time to throw away;
A time to tear,
And a time to sew;
A time to keep silence,
And a time to speak;
A time to love,
And a time to hate;
A time of war,
And a time of peace.

Ecclesiastes 3:1-8

Fresh from the River

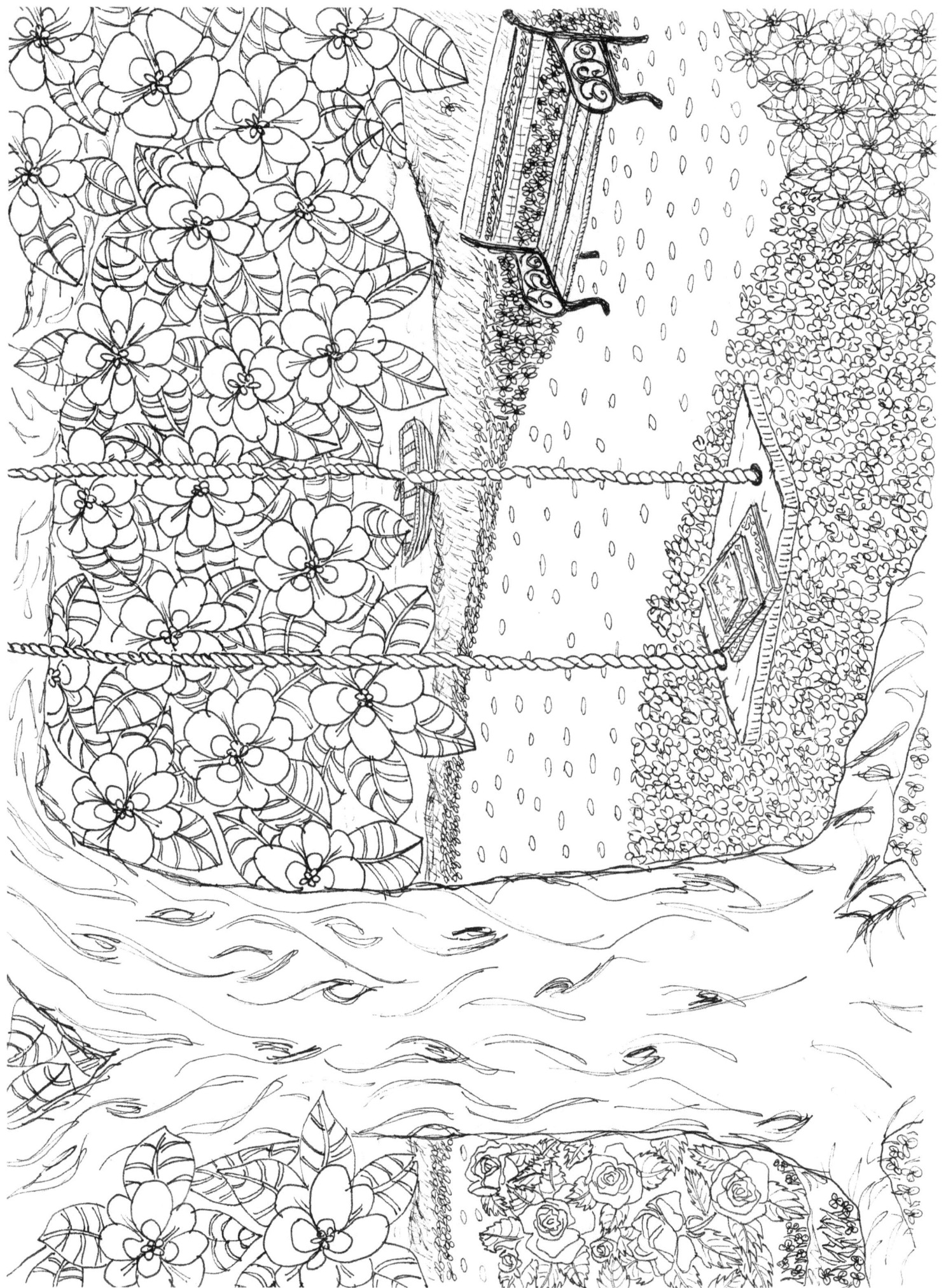

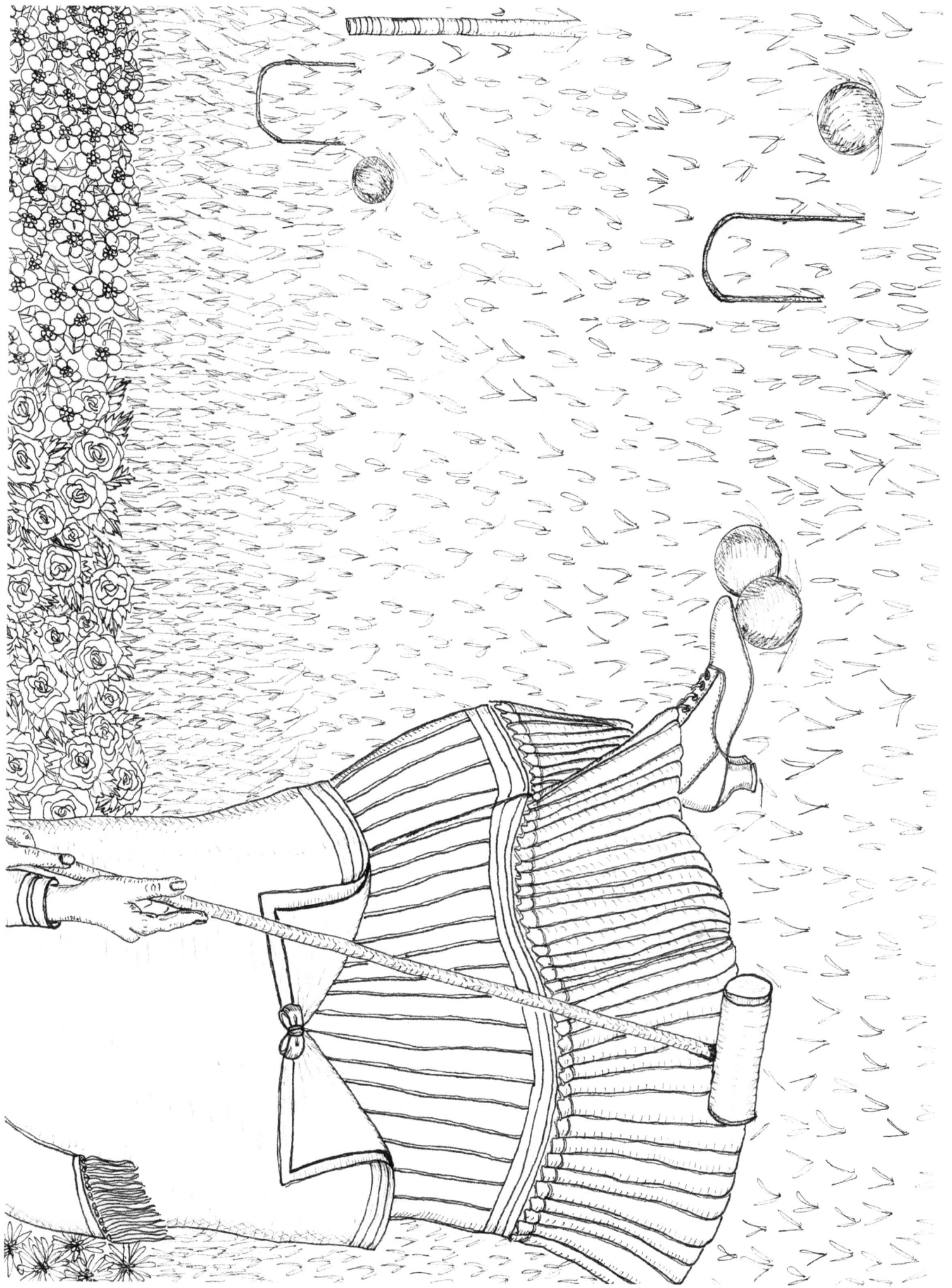

WHAT HAPPENED DURING THIS SEASON OF MY LIFE?

WHAT DID I LEARN IN THIS SEASON?

HOW DID I IMPROVE?

WHAT COULD I HAVE DONE BETTER?

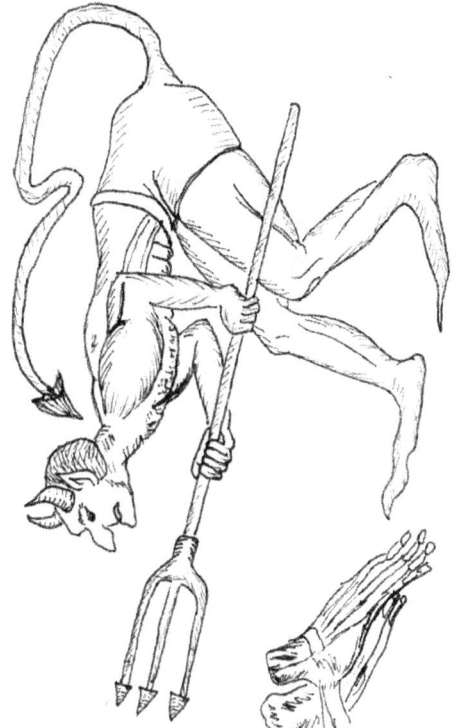

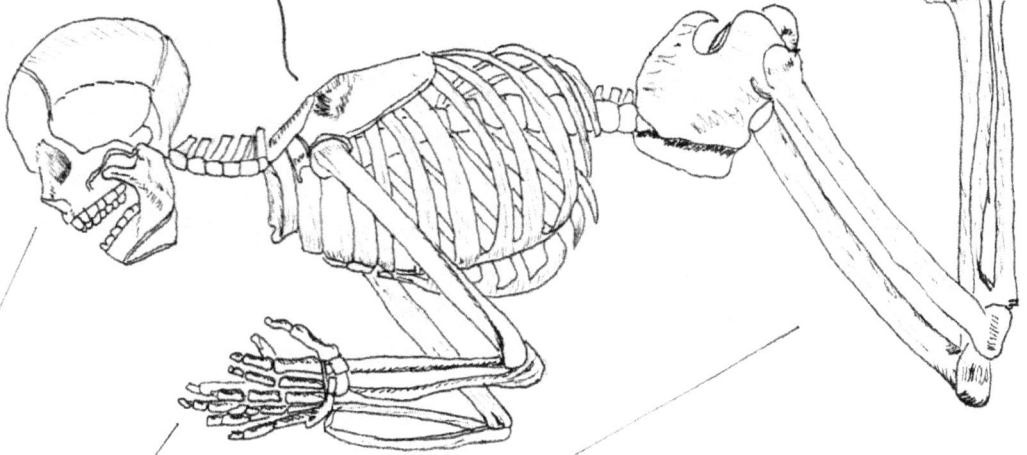

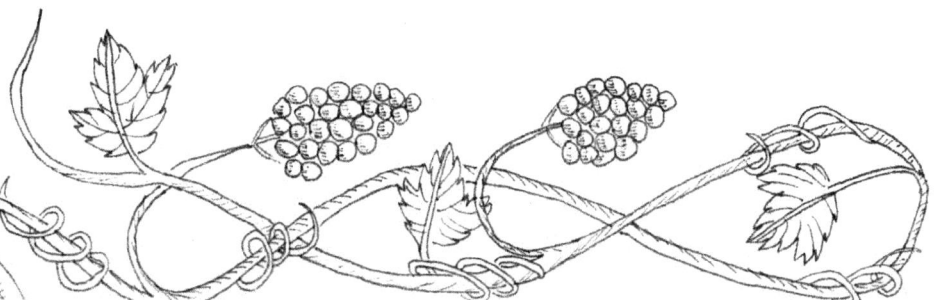

Fine Dining

WHAT HAPPENED DURING THIS SEASON OF MY LIFE?

WHAT DID I LEARN IN THIS SEASON?

HOW DID I IMPROVE?

WHAT COULD I HAVE  DONE BETTER?

_____

_____

_____

_____

_____

_____

_____

_____

_____

_____

_____

_____

WINTER

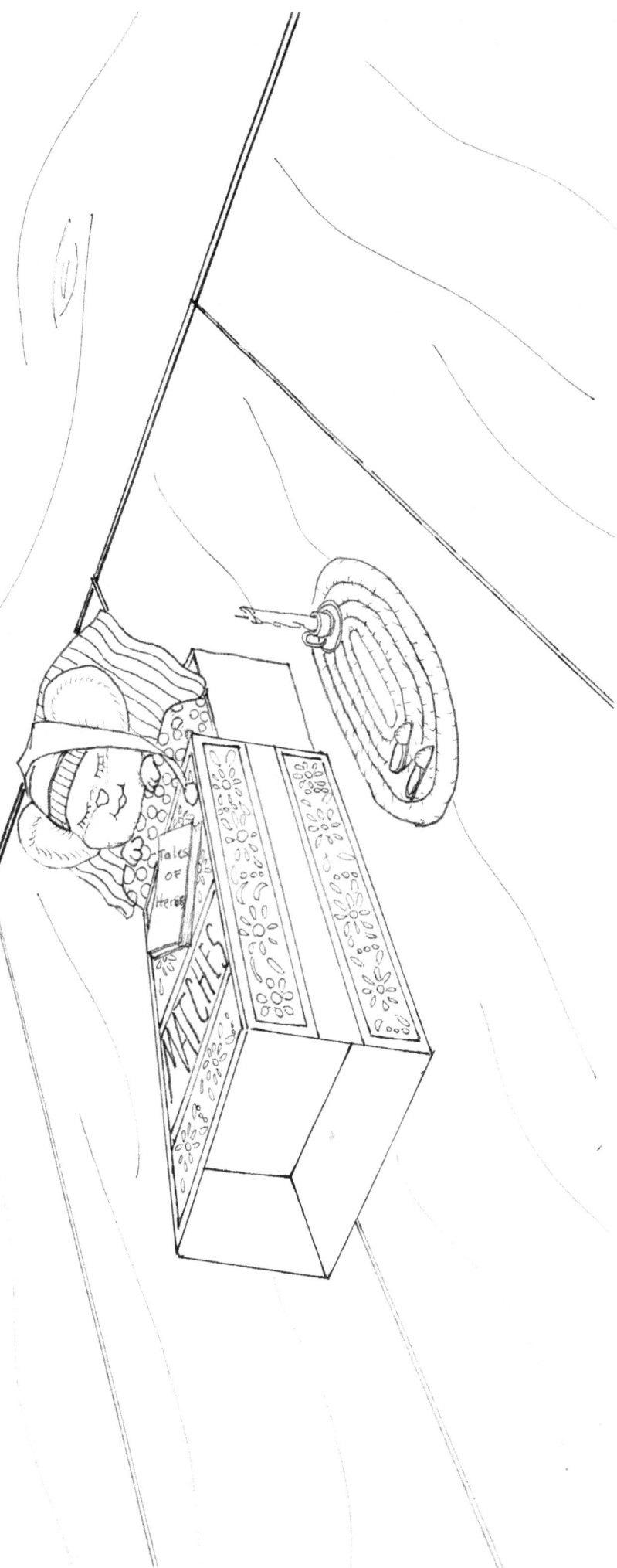

IN WITH THE NEW

I'd like to
LASSO
you for my
VALENTINE,
pardner!

WHAT HAPPENED DURING THIS SEASON OF MY LIFE?

WHAT DID I LEARN

IN THIS SEASON?

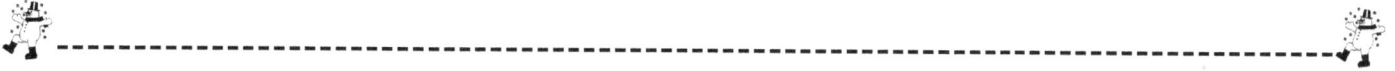

HOW DID I

 # IMPROVE?

WHAT COULD I HAVE DONE BETTER?

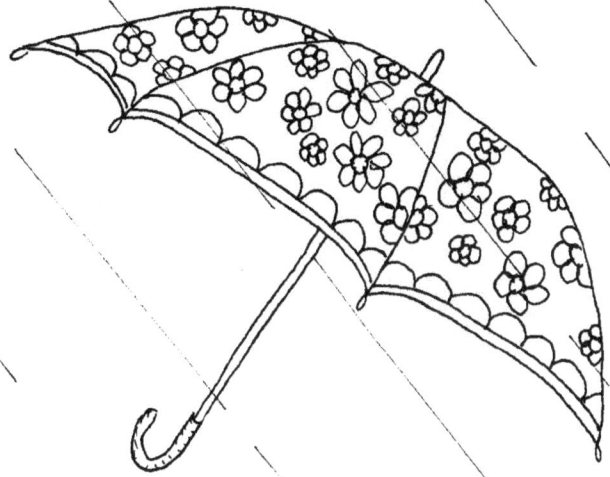

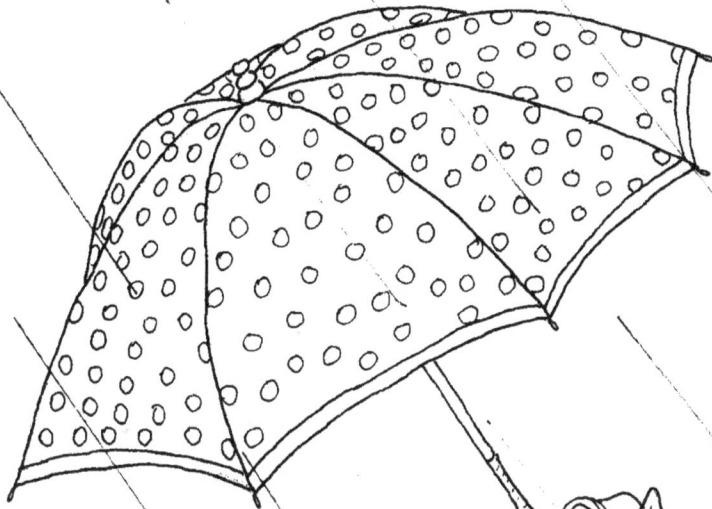

WHAT HAPPENED DURING THIS SEASON OF MY LIFE?

WHAT DID I LEARN IN THIS SEASON?

HOW DID I

IMPROVE?

WHAT COULD I HAVE DONE BETTER?

ABOUT THE AUTHOR

Wendy Yessler was voted most artistic of her senior class at Gwynn Park High School in Brandywine, MD. She illustrated for the school newspaper and designed the covers for band & choir concerts and other school programs. While attending Evangel University in Springfield, MO, she served as Artist for the university bookstore one year. During her university time, she continued to design covers for programs at her former high school as well as design announcements requested by fellow students.

She has two adult children and is currently living on the East Coast in the mountains where she is working on several more projects.

To contact the author, see contact information in front of the book.

www.ingramcontent.com/pod-product-compliance
Lightning Source LLC
Chambersburg PA
CBHW081147040426
42445CB00015B/1795